A FAITH THAT WORKS

A FAITH THAT WORKS

Dr. R. Michael Baldock

Ordering Information:

For orders and inquiries, please contact:
1-888-404-1388
www.goldtouchpress.com
book.orders@goldtouchpress.com

Printed in the United States of America

CONTENTS

INTRODUCTION

Whether we realize it or not, we walk in some kind of faith every day. You may be thinking "how is that?" When you enter into a room and turn on the light switch, you do so with faith, that is, faith in the electrician that he did his job correctly, with the result of the lights coming on. When you start your car, you are expressing a faith in the car manufacturer that it will start and continue to run properly.

Faith is a word that gets loosely tossed around in the Christian circles; however, many are not waking in **"True (The) Faith."** No amount of works that one does will produce faith; however, true faith will produce works (James 2:14-26). ***"I will show you my faith by my works." James 2:18b***

The **"True (The) Faith"** I am speaking of a faith within the correct object, which is, **'Faith in the Cross and the finished Work of Jesus Christ.'** I have discovered after many years of study on the subject of faith, that there is only one kind if faith that pleases God. Again, I am speaking of **'Faith in the Cross and what Jesus Christ accomplished there!'**

Within the following pages, I want to take you, the reader, on a journey of discovery. In the great book of Hebrews, the writer has left us with an entire chapter on what I like to call **"The Heroes of Faith!"**

Upon studying the 11th chapter of Hebrews, we will discover, within the scriptures, an unfolding revelation of the kind of faith it took for all of those recorded in this **"Great Hall of Fame of Faith"** chapter.

While walking in faith, each individual produced works which revealed their faith within receiving and/or embracing the promises of God. We will discover that these did not walk in just any kind of faith. These Heroes revealed a **'true faith,' they looked forward to the Cross and what Jesus Christ would do there, while today, the believer must look back at the Cross and what Jesus Christ accomplished there!**

> *"Wherefore seeing we also are compassed about with so great a cloud of witnesses, let us lay aside every weight, and the sin which doth so easily beset us, and let us run with patience the race that is before us,"*

> *"Looking unto to Jesus The author and Finisher of our faith; who for the joy that was set before Him endured the cross, despising the shame, and is set at the right hand of the throne of God."*

> *"For consider Him that endured such contradiction of sinners against Himself, lest ye be wearied and faint in your minds." Hebrews 12:1-3*

CHAPTER 1

Faith and Works

"Yea, a man may say, Thou Hast Faith,
and I have works: show me thy faith
without thy works, and I will show thee my
faith by my works."
James 2:18

This great Epistle of James has been referred to as the **"New Testament Book of Proverbs."** The main theme in this Epistle is James proclaiming that true faith will be revealed by works. Some were declaring they had faith, yet it was empty faith without any outward signs. There is no amount of work that one can do to receive and walk in faith. Faith, although it comes by hearing the word of God (Romans 10:10), comes with action (James 1:22). James declares that it is time to make our faith known. In other words, it is time to employ outward actions to reveal inward faith.

"What is the use (profit), my brethren, for
anyone to profess to have faith if he has no [good]

> *works [to show for it]? Can [such] faith save [his soul]?" James 2:14 The Amplified Bible*

The above passage of scripture is full of questions that every believer should read carefully. Upon reading them they should examine themselves to determine whether or not he or she walks in "true Faith." Is my faith producing good works? Is my faith one of speech only, rather than a lifestyle? Is my faith one of profession rather than possession?

If your faith is not producing good works, a Christ-like lifestyle, and bringing forth possessions from the word of God, then you are living in what James refers to as **"dead Faith"** (James 2:17, 20, 26), or faith that has no deeds (works) (James 2:14).

In his studies of the Epistle of James, A.T. Robertson refers to dead faith as **"hollow Faith."** Tyndale's New Testament Commentaries on James' Epistle refers to it as **"a wordy faith,"** meaning it is only words with no action. It also is referred to as **"spurious faith"** and **"Christless faith."**

Another amazing revelation in James is his writing to believers rather than non-believers. James is giving the believers a sharp rebuke, declaring *"Faith without works is dead."* In James 2:15-17, he addresses how foolish it is to profess faith without producing works. Notice:

> *"If a brother or sister is poorly clad and lacks food each day,"*

> *"And one of you says to him, Good-bye! Keep [yourself] warm and well fed, without giving*

*him the necessities for the body, what good does
it do?"*

*So also faith, if it does not have works (deeds
and action of obedience to back it up), by itself
is destitute of power (inoperative, dead)."
Amplified Bible.*

Notice in verse 17 the phrase *"So also faith."* The King James
Version of the Bible reads *"Even so faith."* This phrase does
not deny the fact that they had faith; however, their faith was
misplaced, which is the wrong kind of faith. There are two
very distinct ways to determine whether or not the believer is
walking in "true Faith."

1. **Is my faith centered in the Cross and what Jesus
   Christ accomplished there?**

2. **Any kind of faith that does not have the Cross of
   Christ as its object will never produce anything of
   good use.**

The Apostle Paul instructed the Church at Corinth to "To a
self examination in order to determine whether or not they are
professing and walking in **"The Faith."** (2 Corinthians 13:5)

Abraham is a good example of faith producing good works. He
continued to hold onto God's promise for a son, and he did not
waver in his faith. Neither did he consider the deadness of his
body or of Sarah's womb (Romans 4:17-21). For twenty-five
years, he believed and walked in faith. That faith, in the word
spoken by God, produced Isaac. Now his seed is in the sands
on the beaches. Because of his faith and works, it was counted

unto him for righteousness. We will discuss Abraham's faith in greater detail in another chapter. Let's dig a little deeper into what James is saying concerning the right kind of faith.

> ***"Yea, a man may say, Thou hast faith, and I have works: show me thy faith without works, and I will show thee my faith by my works."***
> ***James 2:18***

James makes it very clear that works will always accompany faith. He also states that faith cannot be proven apart from works (faith in action). It is also interesting that James points out that true faith comes from within the believer as an attitude. It is also worth noting that faith in itself cannot be seen; therefore, one can only tell that faith is there when action from the believer takes place. Just a profession of faith proves nothing of its existence; however, when works, deeds, and/or actions are involved, it will reveal true faith. Let's go a step further. The phrase ***"Yea a man may say, thou hast faith, and I have works"*** at first glance seems to imply that faith and works are divided, or a person can have one without the other; however, that is far from the truth. That line of thinking would be laughable if so many had not fallen into that trap. There is simply no such thing as the right kind of faith without the right kind of works. Nor is there the right kind of works without the right kind of faith.

The next phrase James uses to further drive home proper faith and proper works is ***"Show me thy faith without thy works, and I will show thee my faith by my works."*** Again, James proclaims that faith without works is a dead, lifeless, unproductive faith, for it is impossible to show faith without any action. Just because a man may *say* he has faith does not make it so. Notice in the next scripture how James ties this together:

> *"Thou believest that there is one God; thou doest well; the devils also believe, and tremble."*
> *James 2:19*

We must understand that merely believing that there is **"one God"** does not prove that anyone is justified by faith alone. Note that James makes the statement **"The devils also believe and tremble."** It is certainly clear that the devils are not saved simply because they believe in God. This verse also indicates, without argument, that just believing is not the same as having a saving faith. To say **"Thou believest that there is one God,"** is, without a doubt, where millions are at today. The truth is, without the proper (right) kind of faith, they will be as lost as the devils that believe the same thing. Just saying **"I believe"** is not sufficient. In fact, it is one of the roads that will lead to a false salvation. Jesus said *"The thief cometh not, but for to steal, and to kill, and to destroy" John 10:10a.* One of the greatest ways the enemy has found to steak, kill, and destroy is to present a false way to salvation.

Next, in verse twenty, James clears up his previous statements (although it was already very clear) with the following:

> *"But wilt thou know, o vain man, that faith without works is dad?" James 2:20*

This is the second of three times that James uses the phrase **"Faith without works is dead."** The word **"vain"** means *foolish and empty.* In other words, **"How foolish and empty-minded**

is it to remotely think that one can walk in true faith" without works proceeding from it? The next four verses talk about Abraham and his faith; however, as I mentioned earlier, we will go into depth concerning Abraham in another chapter.

The third time James uses the phrase **"Faith without works is dead"** is in verse 26

> *"For as the body without the Spirit is dead, so faith without works is dead also." James 2:26*

It is difficult for me to comprehend how so many can still remain puzzled at what James has taught. Just as the body is dead without the Spirit, so is faith dead without works. This means that faith without works is likened unto a dead corpse which is use-less. Please understand that James was not (nor am I) saying that good works is the beating heart of faith. On the contrary, faith is the life force of a genuine, true, and proper kind of faith. Simply put, you may be obedient without any faith; however, you cannot have real, true faith without obedience. Obedience is the direct result of faith.

In Hebrews chapter twelve, it states:

> *"Therefore Then, since we are surrounded by so great a cloud of witnesses [who have borne testimony to the truth], let us strip off and throw aside every encumbrance (unnecessary weight) and that sin which so readily (defy and cleverly) clinges to and entangles us, and let us run with patient endurance and steady and active persistence the appointed course of the race that is set before us." Hebrews 12:1 Amplified Bible*

Hebrews chapter eleven, which is known as **"The Hall of Fame of Faith,"** is the witnesses that are referred to in the above passage. It is the Old Testament saints that looked forward to what Jesus Christ was going to accomplish at the Cross. In this chapter, the believer is given the ultimate encouragement to live a life of faith. In the first two verses, we are given a wealth of information concerning the ingredients that make faith work. As we begin to look at each ingredient, I want to challenge you, the reader, to examine carefully where you stand in your walk of faith. In the next several chapters, we are going to examine what the true and proper **"Works of Faith"** are, so fasten your seatbelts and let's begin our journey into **"A Faith That Works!"**

CHAPTER 2

True Faith

It is important to understand what kind of faith the **'Great Heroes of Faith'** walked in. As I said in the introduction, without a doubt, I have studied on the subject of faith more than any other subject. When I look back at how I was literally thrown into faith without ever being taught its exact meaning it had to be God in the Person of the Holy Ghost that brought me to this point. I actually went through on the job training in my faith walk. I had several ups and downs, good times and times of great learning! At present, being in my fifty-first year of ministry, I am still learning the **'Walk of Faith.'** When the Holy Spirit opened my eyes and gave me revelation of **'The Faith,'** it changed my walk and relationship with Jesus Christ.

The phrase, **'The Faith'** is mentioned forty times in the King James Version of the Bible. Thirty-two of those times it is directly speaking of **'The Cross and the Finished Work of Jesus Christ.**

Upon studying the 11th chapter of Hebrews, I discovered, within the scriptures, an unfolding revelation of the kind of faith it took for all of those recorded in this **"Great Hall of Fame of Faith"** chapter.

While walking in faith, each individual produced works which revealed their faith within receiving and/or embracing the promises of God. We will discover that these did not walk in just any kind of faith. These Heroes revealed a **'true faith,'** **they looked forward to the Cross and what Jesus Christ would do there, while today, the believer must look back at the Cross and what Jesus Christ accomplished there!**

> *"Wherefore seeing we also are compassed about with so great a cloud of witnesses, let us lay aside every weight, and the sin which doth so easily beset us, and let us run with patience the race that is before us,"*
>
> *"Looking unto to Jesus The author and Finisher of our faith; who for the joy that was set before Him endured the cross, despising the shame, and is set at the right hand of the throne of God."*
>
> *"For consider Him that endured such contradiction of sinners against Himself, lest ye be wearied and faint in your minds." Hebrews 12:1-3*

The phrase, *"Wherefore seeing"* is referring to receiving an understanding of what we have read in the Eleventh Chapter of Hebrews.

The Phrase *"are compassed about with so great a cloud of witnesses"* refers to being surrounded with so many testimonies that this **'Kind of Faith'** works. The *'cloud of witnesses'* is from the Greek word, *'Martus'* meaning; witness. Literally, one who remembers, one who has information or knowledge or joint-knowledge of anything; hence, one who can give information, bring to light, or confirm anything. In Hebrew 12:1 it is a description of witnesses who have experimental knowledge of that which is required of us, which in this case is, **Faith in the Cross and what Jesus Christ Finished there! It is from those who have been there and done that!** There are living witnesses among us today that have proven when the **'object of faith is right, it will work right!'**

The phrase, *"let us lay aside every weight"* referring to anything and all things that weigh heavily upon the believer. (Matt. 11:28-30) This is also written in the *'aorist participle'* which expresses simple action, as opposed to a continuous action of the *'present participle.'* However, it does not in itself indicate the time of action. Therefore, *'laying aside every weight'* is an action that must be done by the believer. That action is to take place the moment one becomes aware of what is hindering them.

The phrase *"and the sin which does so easily beset us"* is speaking of the *'sin nature.'* The Apostle Paul wrote that the believer is to no longer allow the *'sin nature'* to have dominion over them **(Ro. 6:14).**

The phrase, *"that so easily besets us"* is referring to how easy it is for things to hinder and impede the progress of the believer.

The phrase, *"run with patience"* is from the Greek word, *'Hupomone'* from, *'hupo'* meaning under, and *'meno'* to abide. Patience, endurance as to things or circumstances surrounding us.. This word is associated with *'Hope'* **(1 Thess. 1:3)** and refers to the quality that does not surrender to circumstances or succumb under trial.

This is to live your life abiding under and in what *'Jesus Christ did at Calvary!'* It is being steadfast in 'The Faith!' (Hebrews 10:23; 35-38; 1 Peter 5:19)

The phrase, *'the race that is set before us'* is from the Greek word, *'Agon'* which is implying force or violence. Strife, contention, contest for victory or mastery such as to pertaining to the Greek games of running, boxing, and wrestling. Paul plainly uses the word in this fashion (1 Tim. 6:12; 2 Tim. 4:7) and applies the word to the struggles in the Christian life (1 Cor. 9:24) . A race (Heb. 12:1). A struggle, contest, contention, (Phil. 1:30; Col. 2:1; 1 Thess. 2:2).

The Phrase, *"looking unto Jesus"* meaning; to consider attentively, which, is to give all your attention to *'Jesus Christ'* as the object of your faith. The word looking is from the Greek word, *'apharao '* which means; to turn the eyes away from other things and fix them on something. Also it is to turn one's mind to a certain thing. In this case, it is speaking specifically to Jesus Christ. Our mind and eyes should be on Him and what He finished at Calvary

The phrase, *"the author and finisher of our faith" (the Greek text reads "the author and finisher of the faith.")* The word *'author'* is from the Greek word, *'Archegos'* meaning; the beginning or rule. It means originator, founder, leader, chief, prince. Jesus Christ is called the *'archegos'* of life (Acts 3:15); of faith (Heb.12:2); of salvation (Heb. 2:10). **'The Faith'** has its origin in Jesus Christ. He not only walked in faith, He was the supreme example of **'The Faith!**

The word, **'finisher'** is from the Greek word, **'Telelotes'** from **'teleios'** meaning; that which achieves its goal. A completer, perfecter, one who brings something through to the goal so as to win and receive the prize (Heb.12:2).

The phrase, **'the faith'** consists within the life of Jesus Christ and all that He accomplished (finished John19:30) at Calvary (the Cross). Through His Faith we now through the ability of the Holy Spirit walk in **'True Faith with all its benefits!'**

The joy that was before Him was the day of Redemption. It certainly had to be painful to leave the splendor of Heaven and become the Incarnate Son of God to defeat Satan and strip sin from its powerful bite. However, He faced it with joy knowing He would Reconcile man back to God!

> *"Though He needed not that faith by which a sinner is justified, yet in finishing His work on earth, he led His people the way to complete victory over every enemy, by patient, obedient reliance on His Heavenly Father. And, as He had in all things the pre-eminence, so also in sufferings, which He endured for the joy set before Him of the salvation of so many sinners from eternal destruction." Matthew Henry*

The Phrase, *"endured the cross,"* From the Greek word, *'Hupomeno'* meaning; to remain under, that is, to endure or sustain a load of miseries, adversities, persecutions, or provocation in faith and patience.

The Phrase, *' depising the shame"* The word, *'shame'* is from the Greek word, *'aischune'* meaning; disgrace, disfigurement.

> *"And He disregarded the shame and anguish He was called to endure, in life and in death upon this earth, until His undertaking was finished, and He was raised from the dead, and exalted to the right hand of the throne of God."*
> *Matthew Henry*

The question by many is, **"Why this great punishment?"** As horrific as death by a cross was, it was totally necessary for man to be reconciled to God. It was the price for redemption.

> *"Even though He wasn't cursed by God, and because He had never done anything to warrant such a curse; still, He had to be made a curse for us, which means that He took the curse which we should have taken (Gal. 3:13-14) Jimmy Swaggart Bible Commentary on the Book of Hebrews page 745*

The phrase, *"and is set down at the right hand of the throne of God."* This proclamation indicates that His (Jesus Christ) work was finished (John 19:30) in providing salvation, and Him being seated at the right hand of the throne of God indicates He will never have to be crucified again and He occupies a position of preeminence in the Heavens. This being said, it opens up a position for every believer, **Eph. 1:18-23; 2:6.**

The next scripture has in it great importance for the believer and certainly cannot be overlooked.

> *"For consider Him that endured such contradiction of sinners against Himself, lest ye be wearied and faint in your minds" Hebrews 12:3*

Without the *'Cross and the Finished work of Jesus Christ'* being the correct object of our faith, the only path to walk will be one of weariness and faintness of mind!

CHAPTER 3

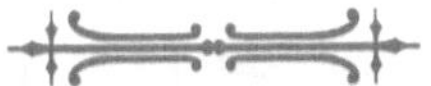

Faith Produces Substance

"Now faith is the substance
(ground of confidence)
of things hoped for,
the evidence of things not seen."
Hebrews 11:1

Before we begin to examine those who put faith to work, let's closely examine the above scripture. In the phrase **"Now faith is the substance,"** the word *substance* comes from the Greek word **Hupostasis,** meaning *to be placed or stand under.* In general, something which has been put under, therefore, is used for a basis or foundation, subsistence or existence, confidence or confident expectation. With this definition in mind, it reveals that faith will bring into and guarantee its existence. This means that faith will materialize (bring substance) even though it cannot be seen in the natural as of yet.

We covered this in the first book of this faith series; however, I believe it bears repeating. With faith being the *"ground of confidence,"* it can also be referred to as ***the title deed.*** Moultan and Millligan, in their "Vocabulary of the Greek Testament" say concerning the usage of this term,

> *"These varied uses are at first sight somewhat perplexing, but in all the cases there is the same central idea of something that underlies visible conditions and guarantees a future possession."*

Matthew Henry gives some incredible insight in his commentary on Hebrews 11:1:

> *"Faith and hope go together; and the same things that are the object of our hope are the objects of our faith."*

> *"It [faith] is affirm persuasion and expectation that God will perform all that He has promised to us in Christ; and this persuasion is so strong that it gives the soul...possession...of these things."*

> *"Believers in the exercise of faith are filled with joy unspeakable and full of glory, Christ dwells in the soul by faith; and the soul is filled with the fullness of God."*

The Preacher's Outline and Sermon Bible states some interesting comments that I believe are worthy for the believer to look upon:

> *Faith is trusting and possessing all that God is and says.*

> *Faith is believing and possessing all that God is and says.*

Faith is having confidence in and possessing all that God is and says.

Faith is hoping for something and possessing it because God exists and has promised it.

Faith Is Not

"I think so, I hope so"
"It may be so; it may not be so."
"It might be true; it might not be true."

Biblical faith does not deal with what is unreal, imaginary, fanciful, visionary, superficial, or deceptive. Biblical faith is the knowledge, experience, and possession of things hoped for. True Biblical faith deals only with truth and reality. It is....

1. Knowing what is real.

2. Experiencing what is real.

3. Possessing what is real

The phrase, **"of things hoped for"** is from the Greek word **Elpizo,** from the word, **Elpis,** meaning *to hope; expect with desire; to hope in the manner of trust, to confide; to set one's hopes upon something that is the hope of future good fortune.*

As we examined the definition of the phrase **"of things hoped for,"** we have discovered that this hope is not something without substance. This statement reveals faith in action (works, deeds). This kind of hope makes unseen things visible and the promises of God present. It is next to impossible to separate **"Faith and Hope"** in this context.

The phrase, **"the evidence of things not seen."** The word **evidence** is from the Greek word **Elegchos,** meaning *conviction*. This word is found only in **2 Timothy 3 :16** and **Hebrews 11:1**. It implies not merely the charge on the basis of which one is convicted, but also the manifestation of the truth of that charge. Our discovery is that faith and hope bring into existence the things that God has promised. Living by faith is not a fruitless life, but a life that makes those things that are not into being. It is taking God at His word and living confidently in it. The Amplified Bible sums it up this way.

<u>Substance and Evidence</u>

Faith is revealed within the *"substance of things hoped for."* And the evidence of one's faith is manifested in the *"substance."* Let's look at a few examples;

In 1 Kings chapter 17;8-24 when Elijah went to Zarepath, God had made preparations for him through a widow woman. Upon Elijah's arrival the woman was gathering sticks and was going to use the last bit of oil and meal to make a cake for her and her and then they were going to wait on death. The Prophet Elijah gave her instructions to feed him first and promised that her meal would not waste and neither would her cruse of oil fail. The woman obeyed the man of God, and moved in faith. The substance and evidence of her faith was revealed when her meal barrel was never empty and her cruse of oil was filled!

Another evidence of this woman's faith came forth when her son died and she called upon Elijah. Elijah stretched himself upon the child and the child was revived!

In Luke Chapter 17:11-19, there were ten lepers who cried out to Jesus to have mercy on them. Jesus responded by telling them to go and present themselves unto the priests. This would not be possible in their condition. However, as they went they were cleansed and when one of them saw that he was healed he turned back to Jesus to glorify God! Jesus said to him, *"Arise go thy way: thy faith hath made thee whole."* His cleansing of leprosy and being made whole was the substance and evidence of his faith!

I personally believe that all of these men when cleansed from leprosy. However, the one man that came back to Jesus was not only cleansed but made whole. I believe, that him, *"being made whole"* was the removal of any evidence of ever having leprosy.

You can see the substance and evidence of faith within those that Jesus touched and healed. So, that answers the question of how one will know if they are walking and living in **'The Faith,'** that is **'Faith in the Cross and the finished work of Jesus Christ,'** look at the substance and evidence in your life. The substance and evidence that I am speaking of, is not in the stuff that we have accumulated but rather the change that has happened and is continuing to take place in our everyday living. I have always said, **"Thank God I am not what I used to be and Thank God I am not yet what I am going to be, He is still working on me!"**

Once again, remember;

> *"Now Faith is the assurance (the confirmation, the title deed) of the things [we] hope for. Being the proof of things [we] do not see and the conviction of their reality [faith perceiving as real fact what is not revealed to the senses] Hebrews 11:1 Amplified Bible*

I believe that this sums it up as well as possible. Faith is far more than just believing, it is a **Lifestyle** for the true believer. Now, go forth in your faith walk and watch the promises of God become reality!

CHAPTER 4

Faith Brings A Good Report

"For by [faith, trust and holy fervor born of faith] the men of old had divine testimony borne to them and obtained a good report."
Hebrews 11:2 Amplified Bible

The **"men of old"** refers to the Patriarchs, Prophets, and Saints in the Old Testament. These great men and women were full of tenacity in their faith walk. Notice in the above scripture what faith birthed within them; trust and holy fervor. These are some elements that are missing in most of today's Christians. Where has the trust and holy fervor gone? Most of it has vanished due to the watered down messages of the **"Modern day Church."**

The Patriarchs, Prophets and Saints of the Old Testament had their faith in the coming Messiah, Jesus Christ, who would become the Supreme Sacrifice. They looked to the day when the **"Finished Work of Jesus Christ at Calvary"** would strip the enemy of his power and render sin powerless (Romans 6:14; Colossians 2:14-15).

These great men and women of old left country and families to follow after the promises of God. They subdued kingdoms, wrought righteousness, obtained promises, and stopped the mouths of lions. They quenched fire, escaped the sword of their enemies, when they were weak they were made strong. They overcame giants and the armies of enemies when they were outnumbered. They witnessed their dead risen, and some were tortured and refused to give way to their oppressors. They were mocked and beaten, and some were stoned while others were sawn asunder. They wandered about in sheepskins and goatskins, being destitute, afflicted, and tormented. They wandered in deserts, mountains, dens, and caves; however, they would not let go of the promises of God that were before them.

It would do for today's believer to examine closely the lives of these "Faith Heroes," especially when so many are turning away from God for the smallest things. A *"Good Report"* comes to those who will hear the Word and begin to obey it.

> ***"But be ye doers of the Word, and not hearers only, deceiving your souls." James 1:22 KJV***

> ***But be ye doers of the Word [obey the message], and not merely listeners to it, betraying yourselves [into deception] by reasoning contrary to the Truth." James 1:22 Amplified Bible***

The phrase ***"be ye doers of the Word"*** is from the Greek word **"Logos,"** deriving from the word **"Lego,"** meaning *to speak, intelligence,* a word as the expression of that intelligence. This speaks of ***"the engrafted word,"*** which is given to promote growth to the believer. Without hearing and obeying the Word, one binds the hands of the Holy Spirit, who is the one that brings growth. Not only does the Word promote growth, when applied it also brings about a change. It is impossible to hear the Word, believe the Word, and do (apply) the Word without being changed. James makes this very clear in the scripture when he said:

> *"Wherefore lay apart all filthiness and superfluity of naughtiness, and receive with meekness the engrafted word, which is able to save your souls." James 1:21*

I am reminded when God spoke to Israel and gave them the road map to the manifestation of His promises.

> *"And it shall come to pass, if thou wilt hearken diligently (to hear with the intention to obey) unto the voice of the Lord thy God, to observe and to do all His commandments which I command thee this day, that the Lord thy God will set thee on high above all nations of the earth."*

> *"And all these blessings shall come on thee, and overtake thee, if thou shalt hearken unto the voice of the Lord thy God." Deuteronomy 28:1-2*

The key to all the blessing of the Patriacrchs of old was to **"Obey the voice of God."** In the Old Covenant, **"Faith"** is demanded, which will lead the believer to a life of obedience. Under the New Covenant, the believer's faith is to have as its object, **"The Cross and what Jesus Christ finished there."** Again, as the Patriarchs of old looked toward what Jesus Christ would accomplish, the believer today is to look back at what has already been accomplished at the **Cross.**

When the object of our faith is correct, the blessings of God will come on the believer and overtake him or her. Hearing the *Word* brings faith (Romans 10:17), while doing (applying) the *Word* allows the Holy Spirit to produce growth in your life (Romans 8).

Many are saying *"I believe and I have faith,"* yet they are not showing the growth and fruit of what they are proclaiming. You, the believer, can say ***"I can show you my faith by the good report (God showing His approval) in my life."*** That good report (showing God's approval) is revealed in the manifestation of becoming Christ-like and walking in the **"Newness of Life"** (Romans 6:4), and being partakers of **"His Divine Nature"** (2Peter 1:4). The reward of (correct) faith is God's approval. The evidence of God's approval is the fulfillment of His promises to the believer, and those promises become a living reality in the one expressing his or her faith. This faith is revealed in the everyday living and experience of the believer.

"I Will Show You My Faith By My Good Report"

CHAPTER 5

Faith Produces An Understanding

"Through faith we understand that the worlds were framed by the Word of God, so that things which are seen were not made of things which do appear." Hebrews 11:2

The above verse is full of information concerning faith and creation. It reveals to the believer that God, himself, operates through the principle of faith. It was through faith that He created the worlds. The faith of God also created the Word, and the Word creates faith in those that will hear. With this being said, let's look further into the above scripture;

The phrase *"Through faith"* reveals that the principle of faith begins with God, for God is faith.

The phrase *"We understand that the worlds were framed by the Word of God"* takes us back to the very beginning, when

God created the Heavens and the earth in Genesis, chapter 1. The word *"understand"* is from the Greek word *Neo,* meaning *to perceive with though, coming into consciousness (the mind) as distinct from the perception of senses; to understand; to know a true fact.* What that is saying is that the knowledge of creation is not understood by our natural senses or reasoning, but instead through the eye of faith. Any understanding of the things of God will only come by faith.

The word *"worlds"* is from the Greek word *Aion.* It refers to an age or time, the material universe, and periods of time as administered by God.

The phrase *"The Word of God"* used here is very interesting in the fact that it is not the usual term *"Logos,"* which is used in expressing the Son of God as the Word of God. This word is from the Greek word *"Hrema,"* meaning a word spoken or uttered, denoting the operative all-powerful word or command of God. From this, we understand, through faith, that what we now see came by the *"Spoken Word of God!"*

The last phrase in this passage of scripture says *"so that things which are seen were not made of things which do appear."* This statement goes beyond any natural understanding. The understanding the believer has is *"Through Faith."*

In his Commentary, Volume 6, page 938, Matthew Henry gives great insight to this passage of scripture;

> *"By faith we understand much more of the formation of the world than ever could be understood by the naked eye of natural reason.*

Faith is not a force upon understanding, but a friend and a help to it. Through faith give us the ability to understand the things concerning the worlds?"

1. *That these worlds were not eternal, nor did they produce themselves, but they were made by another.*

2. *That the maker of the worlds is God; He is the maker of all things.*

3. *That He made the world with great exactness; it was a framed work, in everything duly adopted and disposed to answer its end.*

4. *That God made the world by His word; that is, by His essential wisdom and eternal son, and His active will, saying "Let it be done," and it was done. Psalm 33*

5. *That the world was framed from nothing, out of no pre-existent matter...[by[God, who can call all things that are as if they were, and command them into being these things we understand by faith.*

"The Bible gives us the truest and most exact account of the origin of all things. We are to believe it, and not to wrest or run down the scripture's account of the creation because it does not fit with some fantastic hypotheses of our own, which has been, in some learned but conceited men, the first remarkable step towards infidelity, and has led them into many more."

What all of this is saying is that we must believe that God, out of nothing, created this world and all that is in it. It did not come after what our natural minds try to figure or understand, but it came into existence by the ***Spoken Word of God,"*** and God needs nothing in order to make, frame, and create something. This, we understand **by Faith.** It is not faith based on any scientific findings or beliefs. All that we, the believers, need to understand by faith is the Word of God.

If, through faith, we can truly understand how God created the earth and all that is in it, then all we need is the ***Word of God!"*** We do not have to try and dig any deeper than it already is, just accept as the Word says it. Then you can stand up and say:

"I Will Show You My Understanding By My Faith!

CHAPTER 6

Faith Produces
An Excellent Sacrifice

"By faith Abel offered unto God a more excellent sacrifice than Cain, By which he obtained witness that he was righteous, God testifying of his gifts; and by it he being dead yet speaketh"
Hebrews 11:4

It was **"By Faith"** that Abel offered a more excellent sacrifice than Cain. In the phrase **"By Faith,"** we are able to see the follow-up of verse 3. Since faith is the way in which God operates, then faith must be the way man operates, as well. The only way for man to live his life correctly is by faith. This is the beginning of just how powerful the correct kind of faith is. Faith will cause the believer to make the right sacrifice.

The phrase *"more excellent sacrifice"* refers to the fact that Abel made the correct sacrifice, which was a ***blood offering,*** or the life of a spotless lamb, by pointing to the coming ***Lamb*** *of God,* which was and is *Jesus Christ.* It was not the quantity of Abel's sacrifice that made it better than Cain's. Rather, it was the quality of his sacrifice. This reveals to today's believer, as Abel looked forward to the *Cross, and what Jesus Christ would accomplish there,* that for our faith to be correct, we must look back at the *Cross and the finished work of Jesus Christ.*

Let's examine more in-depth; the word *"sacrifice"* is from the Greek word *"Thusia,"* which is from the word *"thoo,"* meaning *to sacrifice.* Spoken as to the bodies of Christians (Romans 12:1) and of their religious service (1 Peter 2:5), also of their praises of God and works of charity to men (Hebrews 13:15-16); however, as mentioned early, this cannot be just any kind of faith and sacrifice. It must be directed correctly. Matthew Henry described it this way:

"We have set before us some illustrious example of faith in the Old Testament. Abel, by faith, offered a more full and perfect sacrifice than Cain. After the fall, God was worshipped by sacrifices; a worship which is a confession of sin, of the desert of sin, and a profession of faith in a Redeemer, who was to be a ransom for the souls of men."

The proclamation *"by which he obtained witness that he was righteous"* is further evidence that correct (the right kind of) faith, which is directed to Jesus Christ, and Him being our Supreme Sacrifice, is the only path to righteousness. The following phrase, *"God testifying of his gifts;"* is speaking of the fact that the *"lamb"* from Abel was a testimony to the true *"Lamb,"* which is Jesus Christ.

The phrase *"God testifying of His gifts,"* refers to the Sacrifice. Notice that *gifts* is expressed as plural. It refers to the following: Abel's sacrifice was a lamb. Here it was a lamb for one man; in Exodus Chapter 12, it was a lamb for a family; in Leviticus Chapter 16, it was a lamb for a nation, Israel; and in John 1:29, it was a lamb (Christ) for the whole world.

Jimmy Swaggart's Bible Commentary on Hebrews, page 666:

The word, *"gifts"* is from the Greek word **"Doron."** This word is used of gifts given as an expression of honor. Every time Abel made the Sacrifice of a lamb, he was giving honor and praise to God for the coming redemption from sin.

The word *"testifying"* in verse 4 is from the Greek word **"Martureo,"** meaning *to be a witness; to give evidence; to bear record.* In its simplest term, it means that God accepted Abel's sacrifice. The phrase *"and by it he being dead yet speaketh"* refers to the fact that even though the body of Abel is dead, his actions of a correct sacrifice is still yet speaking.

The phrase *"being dead"* is from the Greek word **"Apothnesko,"** meaning *to die.* Literally, *to die off,* but used in the simple meaning of *to die.* To die a natural death applied to both men and animals. Additionally, to be dead to sin, as the truly regenerate are, by having renounced and abandoned it in consequence of their conformity with Christ in His death (Romans 6:2).

What does this all mean for the Christian believer of today? It means that our faith must be exclusively in the *"Cross and the Finished Work of Jesus Christ."* It means that we must be dead to sin in order to walk in the *"Newness of Life"* (Romans

6:4) that Jesus Christ has provided for all that will believe and walk in correct faith.

It also speaks of the believer presenting his or her body as a living sacrifice (Romans 12:1):

> ***"I beseech you therefore brethren, by the mercies of God, that ye present your bodies (make them available) a living sacrifice, holy, acceptable unto God, which is your reasonable service."***

The word ***"living"*** is from the Greek word, **"Zao,"** meaning *to have life* or *to be alive*. It also refers to being alive spiritually; spiritual living. The term ***"zon"*** is used in a trans sense and means not only living, but *causing to live; vivifying; quickening."*

The word ***"sacrifice"*** is from the Greek word **"Thusia,"** which is the same word used in Hebrews 11:4 concerning Abel's Sacrifice, speaking of the bodies of Christians. The phrase ***"Living Sacrifice"*** in Romans 12:1 can only be accomplished through the work of the Holy Spirit and that is only if we place our faith in the **"Cross"** and **"Jesus Christ,"** for that is the Gospel that brings salvation (1 Corinthians 1:17-18).

This demand for the believer becoming a living sacrifice will only come from the quickening of the Holy Spirit. It must be ***"holy"*** (separated from sin and separated to God) which is all that God will accept, realizing that we no longer belong to ourselves because we are now the temple of God (1 Corinthians 3:16).

To conclude with Romans 12:1, note that being a living sacrifice is ***"your (our) reasonable service."*** The word *"reasonable"* is from the Greek word **"Logikos."** In Romans 12:1, it is the reasonable service or worship to be understood as the service to God, which implies intelligent meditation or reflection without heathen practices.

I believe that this can best be seen by the believer, denying himself, taking up his cross and following Jesus Christ (Luke 9:23). To deny oneself, means, to put a stop to working in one's own ability, strength, knowledge and wisdom, and all the while, taking up the victory that Jesus Christ has provided.

So, when someone says they have faith, you can say;

I Will Show You My Faith By a More Excellent Sacrifice!

That is placing all of my trust, faith and confidence in the Cross and the Finished work of Jesus Christ!

CHAPTER 7

Faith Pleases God

*"By faith Enoch was translated that he should
not see death;
and was not found, because God had
translated him:
for before his translation he had this testimony
that he pleased God."*
Hebrews 11:5

Years ago when I read this passage of scripture, the statement **"he pleased God"** gained my attention. It was one of those times when you are reading and something leaps from the page and creates an intense interest. It was then that I had to dig in to find how and what Enoch did to please God.

The Amplified Bible reads this way;

*"Because of faith Enoch was caught up and
transferred to heaven, so that he did not have a
glimpse of death; and he was not found, because*

> *God had translated him. For even before he was*
> *taken to heaven, he received testimony [still on*
> *record] that he had pleased and been satisfactory*
> *to God." [Genesis 5:21-24}*

Enoch being translated to heaven was due to his depth of faith (he was one of only two men to have this experience, the other being the Prophet Elijah, 2 Kings 2:11). However, what did he do while walking in faith that caused this great event?

In Genesis 5:21-24 most Bible scholars believe that Enoch turned his life over to God at the age of 65. He spent the next 300 years walking and talking with God. He was 365 years old when God translated Him. There is also indication that Enoch was a very popular man. We do know that he was referred to in Luke 3:37 in the genealogy of Jesus. He is also referred to in the book of Jude, verse 14. It is interesting to note, according to Jude 14, that he prophesied of the second coming of Jesus Christ.

> *"And Enoch also, the seventh from Adam,*
> *prophesied of these things, saying, Behold the*
> *Lord cometh with ten thousand of His saints,"*
>
> *"To execute judgment upon all, and to convince*
> *all that are that are ungodly among them of all*
> *their ungodly deeds which they have ungodly*
> *committed, and of all their hard speeches which*
> *ungodly sinners have spoken against Him."*
> *Jude 14-15*

The above text proves without any doubt that Enoch's faith was centered on the **"Cross,"** and what **"Jesus Christ would**

accomplish." So, all indications are that Enoch Prophesied concerning the **"Second Coming of Jesus Christ"** for some 300 years. With sin abounding upon the earth, Enoch continued his walk of faith and communion with God.

So many over the years have asked God the question, **"What does it take to please you?"**

God answered this very question to Israel recorded in the Book of Micah;

> *"Will the Lord be pleased with thousands of rams or ten thousands of rivers of oil? Shall I give my firstborn for my transgression, the fruit of my body for the sin of my soul?"*
>
> *"He hath showed thee, O man, what is good; and what doth the Lord require of thee, but to do justly, and to love mercy, and to walk humbly with thy God?" Micah 6:7-8*

It is evident that Israel had lost sight of what was required of them to please God. Israel had held onto the idea that scarifying was the way God offered salvation, which is just not true. Notice in the scriptures how Israel's thinking was *"I will do more,"* which indicates they were thinking in the realm of quantity rather than quality, believing that this would deliver them from the *"sin of their soul."*

In verse 8, God challenges them look back into the book of Deuteronomy 10:12, where God gave specific instructions on what He required of them.

"And now, Israel, what doth the Lord thy God require of thee, but to fear the Lord thy God, to walk in all His ways, and to love Him, and to serve the Lord thy God with all thy heart and all thy soul." Deuteronomy 10:12

Let's examine all of these requirements;

1. **"To Fear the Lord thy God:"** Fear is from the Hebrew word **"Yare."** There are two main types of fear described by *yare;*

   A. The emotional and intellectual anticipation of harm; what one feels may go wrong for him.

   B. A very positive feeling of awe, or reverence for God, which may be expressed in piety or formal worship. The latter of these two are being referred to in Deuteronomy 10:12.

2. **'To walk in all His ways;"** from the Hebrew word **"Dherekh"** meaning *a going; walk; journey; way; path; road; mode; manner;course; wy of life; lot in life; worship.* More often it refers to the actions and behavior of men. This is a great statement in the fact that it reveals how God expects man to behave.

3. **"And to love Him;"** from the Hebrew word **"Ahav,"** meaning *to love, desire, delight, like, be fond of, covet, or to be passionate.* It implies an ardent and vehement inclination of the mind and a tenderness of affection at the same time. One special use of this word, ***"ahav,"*** is

for the close ties of friendship. God is looking for every believer to enter into a friendship with Him.

4. **"To serve the Lord thy God with all thy heart;"** from the Hebrew word **"Avad,"** meaning *to serve, to worship, to be caused to worship.* The service may be directed toward things, people or God. In this case, it is a worship of honor to God.

5. **"And with all thy soul,"** from the Hebrew word **"Nephesh,"** meaning *a breathing creature.* It is the soul in which the body lives. Another important meaning is life, which is the vital principle in death when it leaves the body. While the soul is presently within the body then must also serve the Lord. That is one reason why the Apostle Paul said to ***"Present your bodies a living sacrifice" Romans 12:1.***

King David wrote, in Psalms 69:30-31, another aspect to pleasing God;

> ***"I will praise the Name of God with a song, and I will magnify Him with thanksgiving."***

> ***"This also shall please the Lord better than an ox or bullock that has horns and hoofs."***

When we raise our voices in songs of praise and thanksgiving, it pleases the Lord. The writer of Proverbs added a new dimension of the results of pleasing God.

"When a man's ways please the Lord, he makes even his enemies to be at peace with him." Proverbs 16:7

This is not saying that your enemies will become your friends or stop being an enemy. However, with one's way being pleasing to the Lord, your enemies recognize the presence of God in your life and back away.

With all of this being said, there is only one true way to please God;

"But without faith (true, honest, correct faith, that is faith in the correct object) it is impossible (it will never happen no matter what a person may do) to please Him; for he that cometh to God must believe (believing is a work of faith, it is what faith does) that He is a rewarder of them that diligently seek Him." Hebrews 11:6 Emphasis mine

The writer of Hebrews makes it very plain in the above scripture that *"Without Faith it is impossible to please."* I have said it in several places in this book; your Faith must be focused on the right object. No one can do enough works to gain salvation, to keep salvation and please God. Everything within the scriptures that we have shared, when it comes to pleasing God, will manifest when faith is right. Faith in the *"Cross and the Finished work of Jesus Christ"* is the foundation of those who walk in correct faith.

> *"But ye beloved, building up yourselves on your most holy faith, praying in the Holy Ghost."*
> *Jude 20*

The phrase, *"most holy faith"* is from the Greek word **"Hagios,"** meaning *sanctified, set apart, consecrated.*

The Apostle Paul sums it, making it plain concerning how to walk in one's life:

> *"I am crucified with Christ; nevertheless I live; yet not I, but Christ liveth in me; and the life which I now live in the flesh I live by the faith of the Son of God, who loved me, and gave Himself for me." Galatians 2:20*

The phrase *"the faith of the Son of God"* is pointing directly to what Jesus Christ did at the cross. There cannot be any speculation concerning what Paul was saying. For a person to please God, it is only in the *"Cross and what Jesus Christ accomplished there."* Now you can say;

<u>I Will Show You My Faith By Pleasing God!</u>

CHAPTER 8

Faith Produces A Reverent Worship and the Fear of the Lord!

"By faith Noah, being warned of God of things not seen as yet, moved with fear, prepared an ark to the saving of his house; by the which he condemned the world, and became heir of the righteousness which is by faith" Hebrews 11:7

Noah's faith is often referred to as *"A Fearful and Reverent Faith."* There certainly is a wealth of information concerning this great *"Man of God."* In the midst of a perverse ungodly world, Noah stood tall. The scriptures declare Noah as one who found *"Grace"* in the eyes of the Lord (it is important to note that this is the first time in scripture that *"Grace"* is mentioned) (Genesis 6:8). He was just and perfect, meaning he was righteous and blameless in his generation. He also walked with God, that is to say, he had continual fellowship with God (Genesis 6:9).

There is much to learn of this kind of faith and what it produces. Remember, we are talking about *"A Faith That Works."*

"By faith Noah, being warned of God of things not seen as yet," means that God spoke (revealed) to Noah concerning things which had never been seen before. Because of the wickedness of man, and their every thought and imaginations continually increasing with evil, God was going to send judgment. This judgment was going to be sent with such intensity that man, the fowl of the air, and the beast of the field would not survive. The only survivors would be within the Ark that Noah was to build.

Upon God speaking to Noah, he *"moved with fear."* The word *"fear"* in this case is not the kind of fear that brings fright. This *"fear"* comes from the Hebrew word **"Eulabeomai,"** meaning *to act cautiously, circumspectly, to reverence, and to stand in awe.* I dare say, this kind of fear is not present today like I have seen it in the past. There is certainly not the reverence that I was taught as a child. Noah moved with reverence and in awe of God.

Let's take a closer look at the importance of the phrase *"moved with fear."* We have already defined what it means to be *"moved with fear."* Let's take it a step further and examine what this kind fear (faith) produces:

> *"The reverent fear and worshipful awe of the Lord [include] the hatred of evil: pride, arrogance, the evil way, and perverted and twisted speech I hate." Proverbs 8:13 Amplified*

I deeply love how the above scripture reveals the evidence of one walking in a faith that produces a *"Reverent Awe of God."*

So, it can be said, **"I will show you my faith by my reverent worship to God, which produces a hatred of evil, pride, arrogance, the evil way, and perverted and twisted speech I hate!"**

There are very few in the Church world today that can make the above claim. There are too many living a compromised lifestyle. This is evident in what is being produced from the "Modern Day Church." There is little separation from sin and separation to God.

> *"The reverent and worshipful fear of the Lord is the beginning (the chief and choice part) of Wisdom, and the knowledge of the Holy One is insight and understanding." Proverbs 9:10 Amplified Bible*

Did you notice what reverent, worshipful fear of the Lord Produces?

1. **The beginning of Wisdom.**

2. **Knowledge of the Holy One.**

3. **Insight and understanding.** The Holy Spirit reveals that any wisdom, knowledge or understanding without the *"Fear of the Lord"* is unproductive.

Again, **"I will show you my faith by walking in the Fear of the Lord which brings Wisdom and knowledge along with insight and understanding of the things of the Lord!"**

> *"The reverent and worshipful fear of the Lord prolongs one's days, but the years of the wicked shall be made short." Proverbs 10:27 Amplified Bible*

What a promise for those who will walk in a **"reverent and worshipful fear of the Lord."** Their days are prolonged!

> *"Reverent and worshipful fear of the Lord is a fountain of life, that one may avoid the snares of death." Proverbs 14:27 Amplified Bible (See also, John 4:7- 14)*

Another great promise for those who walk in *"reverent worshipful fear of the Lord,"* is that it produces a fountain (well) of everlasting life. Jesus spoke to the woman at the well, telling her He had a well of **"Living Water,"** and everyone that drinks from His well will never thirst again. The fear (reverent worship) of the Lord brings access to that well of *"Living Water!"*

> *"The reverent and worshipful fear of the Lord brings instruction, in wisdom, and humility comes before honor." Proverbs 15:33 Amplified Bible*

His well will never thirst again. The fear (reverent worship) of the Lord bring access to that well of **"Living Water!"**

> *"The reverent and worshipful fear of the Lord brings instruction, in Wisdom, and humility comes before honor." Proverbs 15:33 Amplified Bible*

Just as Noah, walking in the *"Fear of the Lord"* received instruction in wisdom, so shall the believer of today. So the believer can say,

"I will show you my faith by walking in the instructions of the Lord, manifesting in wisdom and humility!"

> *"The reverent, worshipful fear of the Lord leads to life, and he who has it rests satisfied; he cannot be visited with [actual] evil." Proverbs 19:23 Amplified Bible (see also, Job 5:19; Psalms 91:3; Proverbs 12:13; Isaiah 46:4; Jeremiah 1:8; Daniel 6:27; 2 Timothy 4:8)*

With the scriptural evidence provided, it is very clear what walking the "Proper Faith' will produce. While Noah was walking toward the promises of God, the believer today is to look back at the many promises that Jesus Christ fulfilled (made available) through the Cross and His resurrection.

Noah's faith put him in position to;

1. **Being warned of God.**

2. **Prepare (a faith that works produces preparation for what is ahead) an Ark for the safety [salvation] of his family.**

3. **To build.**

Noah's faith also had a threefold reward;

1. **His family was saved.**

2. **His faith was vindicated.**

3. **He was counted righteous. He became the heir of righteousness, which came *(comes) faith*.**

The works of Noah's faith was evident by;

1. **Walking in a reverent, worshipful Fear of the Lord.**

2. **His prompt obedience and diligence taking God at his Word.**

3. **His continual standing in the face of those mocking him.**

4. **His looking to the promised seed of a Savior (looking to the Cross)!**

<u>I will Show you my Faith by:</u>

"Walking in the fear of the Lord"

"Having all my faith, hope and trust in The Cross and the *Finished Work of Jesus Christ*"

"By my 'Obedience' to the Word which is produced through Faith"

"By being prepared"

"By putting the Kingdom of God first" Matthew 6:33

CHAPTER 9

Faith Produces Immediate Action

"By faith Abraham, when he was called to go out into a place which he should after receive for an inheritance, obeyed; and he went out, not knowing whither he went." Hebrews 11: 8

In this chapter we are going to examine the faith of Abraham. Abraham's faith is often referred to, *"Obedient and Hopeful Faith."*

When God spoke to Abram (Abraham) in Genesis 12, the depth of his faith was revealed. God was calling him out of his country of Ur of the Chaldees, who were a people that worshipped strange gods. Yet, Abraham's faith was what I like to refer to as an **"Immediate Obedient Faith."** He left his country, family (except Lot), and friends to follow the spoken Word of God not knowing where he was going at the time. His faith was one that, in the natural sense, was risky; however, that is what faith will do. His faith also was one relying and resting totally on the

Word of God. His trust and faith was not subjective, but was objective and rooted within the Word that God spoke.

I am convinced that Abraham, acting **"immediately"** without hesitation, is an important key to walking in true faith. Let me explain. So often, when a person hears the voice through His Word (the Bible), or through a song or statement, they drag their feet trying to decide *should I go or stay?* That was not a problem for Abraham. Abraham's faith was an **"Immediate Obedient Faith."** One of the works of faith is , **"Obedience;"** however, obedience does not create faith. Faith creates obedience. In other words, **"I will show you my faith by my Obedience!"**

This kind of faith could also be referred to as **"Abandonment Faith."** He left behind all distraction from his past and present. This reveals a challenge to every believer today. So many are being held back or distracted because of their past or current situations. It is time to let go of the (your) past and turn your current situations over to God and begin to walk in **"Immediate, Abandonment Faith!**

One of the best descriptions of Abraham's faith is recorded by the Apostle Paul in the great book of Romans.

> ***"Who against hope believed in hope, that he might become the father of many nations, according to that which was spoken, so shall thy seed be." Romans 4:18***

Note that when hope was against him, he yet believed in hope. The word *"hope"* here is from the Greek word **"Elpis,"** meaning *hope desire of some good with expectation of obtaining it.* This hope that Abraham was holding onto was the promise of him becoming the father of many nations, beginning with the birth of Isaac. When God spoke to Abraham and gave him this promise he was approximately seventy-five years old. So, this was not an obedient faith just "hoping" God will come through. Rather, it was faith with a confident hope with a surety that God will perform what He said. It is not **"I hope so,"** but rather **I Know so!"** I call this, **"Visionary Faith."** It is a faith that looks beyond the impossibilities and sees the possibilities.

> *"And being not weak in faith, he considered not his own body now dead, when he was about a hundred years old, neither the deadness of Sarah's womb." Roman 4: 19*

The phrase *"And not being weak in faith"* comes from the Greek word, **"Astheneo,"** meaning; *without strength; weak; powerless; spiritually weak.*

Abraham did not arrive at this place in faith easily. He certainly had his times when compromise and fear gripped him. He lied about Sarah not being his wife because of fear, Genesis 12. He compromised by taking Hagar to bring forth a son, the result of which was the birth of Ishmael, Genesis 16.

It is evident the faith walk is not one for the faint hearted, nor is it without its ups and downs and trials. However Abraham came to the place where he became strong in his faith resulting in strong faith.

"He staggered not at the promise of God through unbelief; but was strong in faith, giving glory to God." Romans 4:20

I want you to noticed two very important statements in Romans 4:19 and 4:20. These statements reveal Abraham's arrival in his faith walk.

1. **He did not considered the deadness of his body nor the deadness of Sarah's womb, verse 19.**

2. **He did not stagger (waver) at the promises of God, through unbelief.** Both of these statements are extremely important in Abraham's faith walk. Abraham came to the place where outside circumstances did not get in the way of his faith. Not only did he walk in **Strong Faith,"** he also became **"Strong in his Faith."** In the great book of James, we are told to avoid wavering or staggering in our faith.

   "But let him ask in faith, nothing wavering. For he that wavereth is like a wave of the sea driven with the wind and tossed."

   For let not that man think that he shall receive anything of the Lord."

   "A double minded man is unstable in all his ways." James 1:6-8

It certainly goes without saying that there are multitudes of situations and circumstances that try to derail one's walk of faith. For the believer, their eyesight must be singular. What I mean by that statement is faith must be totally focused on the **"Cross and what Jesus Christ accomplished there."**

Going back to Abraham for a moment, the last thing I want to examine is in the following passage of scripture;

> *"And being fully persuaded that, what He had promised, He was able also to perform."*
> *Romans 4:21*

The phrase *"fully persuaded"* is from the Greek word **"Plerophoreo,"** meaning; *completely assured or totally convinced.*

This is speaking of the place Abraham came to in his faith walk. Being confronted with his past mistakes, with the inability in own body and the inability of Sarah's body to bring forth a child, was minimal when compared to the power in the promise of God. This is the result of *"A Work of Faith!"*

When you reach this kind of faith, you can stand tall and say, **"I will show you my Faith by not being weak or, staggering but being fully persuaded in all that God says!"** This can be accomplished by placing one's faith exclusively in **"The Cross and the Finished Work of Jesus Christ."**

CHAPTER 10

Faith Produces Strength To Conceive

"Through faith also Sarah herself received strength to conceive seed, and was delivered of a child when she was past age because judged Him faithful Who had promised." Hebrews 11:11

Just as Abraham came to the place of being strong in his faith, so did Sarah. There are two every important statements made concerning Sarah and her faith that I want to examine. The first one is; ***"Through faith Sarah herself received strength to conceive seed."***

Sarah had grown substantially from the first time that she received word that she was going to have a son (Genesis 18:11-13). From the very beginning, Sarah was faced with a natural impossibility with her age and the deadness of her womb. The phrase **"received strength to conceive"** relates to the fact that there was a struggle (fight) involved. It is obvious that the strength to conceive came from God, Himself. However, that was the direct result of her faith in what God had promised.

The only reason I mentioned a struggle is because how hard Satan comes against the believer trying to remove them from their faith. Sometimes it is not removing one totally from faith, but having their faith focused on the wrong thing. I remember a few years ago having my faith life fully tested. I have studied on faith, without a doubt, more than any other subject in the Word of God. God began to speak to me through a teaching that I was listening to, concerning true and proper faith. I thought that I knew faith forward and backwards, but I was in for a surprise. You see, my faith walk used to be in what God can do and what God will do. You may be thinking, **"What is wrong with that?"** The greatest wrong was I had placed my faith on the wrong object. Don't misunderstand what I mean by placing my faith on the wrong object. I still believe in what God can and will do; however, through some great teaching and revelation I was taken deeper into faith and what it really is and how it really works. My faith now is completely focused on the **"Cross and the Finished Work of Jesus Christ!"** Everything that God will do or does is within the cross and what Jesus Christ accomplished there. Whatever one has need of, they can find it in the cross. The cross is the means and Jesus Christ is the source of all that one will ever need.

When Sarah got her faith right she received strength to conceive and birth a child. When your faith is on the right object, you too will be able to conceive and give birth to the promises of God in your life.

The Apostle Paul made a resounding statement concerning his faith walk;

> *"I can do all things through Christ which strengthen me." Philippians 4:13*

This great Apostle came to this place in his walk of faith because he set the object of his right. His faith was not without facing problems and difficulties; however, he stayed focused on the correct object. Notice the following;

> *"I am crucified with Christ: nevertheless I live; yet not I, But Christ liveth in me: and the life which I now live in the flesh I live by the faith of the Son of God, who loved me, and gave himself for me." Galatians 2:20*

Did you notice how Paul said he lives his life? He lives by **"The Faith"** of **"Jesus Christ."** The term, **"The Faith"** refers to the **"Cross and what Jesus Christ accomplished there."** It could be said this way; *"I live my life by the faithfulness of Jesus Christ and what He has accomplished for me!"*

I realize that I have repeatedly referred to the cross and the finished work of Jesus Christ. I am not trying to be redundant; however, I am trying to point every believer to the correct object of faith, without which it becomes impossible to conceive and give birth to the promise of God.

The second thing to notice about Sarah is *"she judged God faithful in what He promised."* Sarah was now facing an impossible situation. She has been barren all of her life. Now she is 90 years old and Abraham is 100. But rather than looking at the surrounding circumstances, she *"judge God faithful."* How can one judge God?

Whether you are aware of it or not, you are judging God every day by your lifestyle. If you are walking in this Christian life you either show God faithful or faithless. It is on display for everyone to see. The way you walk, the way you talk, and those you hang around is revealing your character. Also, when your faith is in anything other than the, **"Cross and what Jesus Christ Accomplished there,"** you are actually judging God as being unfaithful in what He promises.

The question we must ask ourselves is *"are we walking by our own sight or are we walking by faith?"*

> *"For we walk by faith, not by sight:"*
> *2 Corinthians 5:7*

The next question is; *Are you in a place where the Holy Spirit can impregnate you with the gifting, ability and vision that God wants in your life? Will you present yourself unto God and fulfill the calling He has in you?*

In my many years of ministry I have witnessed so many people abort what God had placed within them. Many have fallen prey to the tactics of Satan and failed to accomplish what God had called them to do. When I started in the ministry, I felt impregnated by the Holy Spirit. Through the years we have been able to birth the things God has placed within this ministry. Today, I am still impregnated with the things of God and in the birthing stage. However, let me say, none of this would have been possible without the *'Baptism in the Holy*

Ghost' and the 'Cross and the Finished Work of Jesus Christ' being the object of my faith!

Once again, the believer is instructed to live his or her life by faith and not by their surrounding circumstances. I like to call this ***"Living from the inside out and not the outside in!"***

If you allow the many things that can surround you to disturb your faith in Christ, you will never arrive to make the impossible, possible! You then can stand and say;

I Will Show You My Faith By The Strength to Conceive the Promises of God and Give Them Birth!

CHAPTER 11

A Faith That Forsakes the World

"By faith Moses, when he was come to years, refused to be called the son of Pharaoh's daughter."

"Choosing rather to suffer affliction with the people of God, than to enjoy the pleasures of sin for a season."

"Esteeming the reproach of Christ greater riches than the treasures in Egypt: for he had respect unto the recompense of the reward." Hebrews 11:24-26

While being raised in the household of Pharaoh, at the age of 40 Moses refused to be called the son of Pharaoh's daughter. According to the great Jewish historian, Moses was about five years old when he was adopted and began his education as the son of Pharaoh's daughter. The writer of the book of Acts records the education and position that Moses had in Egypt.

> *""And Moses was learned in all the wisdom of the Egyptians, and was a mighty in words and in deeds." Acts 7:22*

As stated earlier, at the age of 40 Moses makes a decision that would change his life forever.

> *"And when he was full forty years old, it came into his heart to visit his brethren the children of Israel."*

> *"And seeing one of them suffer wrong, he defended him, and avenged him that was oppressed, and smote the Egyptian." Acts 7:23-24*

It was this action that caused Moses to flee Egypt. At this point, Moses chose to suffer affliction with the people of Israel rather than enjoy the pleasures of sin. This certainly is not the state of many today that call themselves Christian. There are so many things of the world that has infiltrated the modern day Church that it is often difficult to tell the believer from the non-believer. Instead of abstaining from the world, the world has been embraced by many so-called Christians and church leaders of today.

Moses spent the next forty years on the backside of the desert before God called and sent him back into Egypt to deliver Israel from the oppressors. The faith of Moses can be put into several categories.

1. **A Sacrificial Faith;** While in Egypt and in the household of Pharaoh, he had everything that a person could want. He had the best of education and knowledge. He had

all the wealth and fame one could ever desire. He had untold possessions and land. He had power and authority. He held a high position, which gave him purpose and responsibility. He had all that most modern Christians strive for, especially with today's message of prosperity. However, Moses chose to suffer along with his brethren rather than to enjoy sin for a season. Note that sin and its enjoyment does not last forever. **It has a payday!**

The Expositor's Greek Testament states it this way;

> *"The significance and source of this refusal lay in his preferring to suffer ill usage with God's people rather than to have a short-lived enjoyment of sin.....it was because they were God's people, not solely because they were of his blood, that Moses threw in his lot with them. It was this that illustrated his faith. He believed that God would fulfill His promise to His people, little likelihood as at present there seemed to be of any great future for his race. On the other hand there was....the enjoyment which was within his reach if only he committed the sin of denying his people and renouncing their future as promised by God" (Marcus Dods. The Epistle to the Hebrews. "The Greek Expositor's Testament." Vol. 14, ed, by W. Robertson Nicoll, Grand Rapids, MI: Eerdmans, 1970, p. 360).*

2. **An Expectant Faith;** Moses chose the sufferings of Christ, the promised seed of the Savior over the riches of Egypt. He considered God's reward to be far greater than anything this world had to offer. This is the same

position that every believer should find themselves in today. While Moses looked toward the Cross of Christ, we are to look back at the Cross and what Jesus Christ accomplished there.

William Barclay notes the experience of Moses and what he did this way;

> *"Moses was the man who gave up all earthly glory for the sake of the people of God. Christ gave up His glory for men. He became despised and rejected: He abandoned the glory of Heaven for the buffets and the scourging and the shame inflicted by men. Moses, in his day and generation, shared in the sufferings of Christ. Moses was the man who chose the loyalty that led to sufferings rather than the ease which led to earthly glory. He would rather suffer for the right than enjoy luxury with the wrong. He knew that the prizes of earth were contemptible compared with the ultimate reward of God"* **(The Letter to the Hebrews, p. 178).**

I believe that Barclay states it correctly. The trouble with today's modern message is that both the world and the spiritual things of God can be mingled. That is simply not true. It must be one or the other.

3. **An Enduring Faith;** An **"Enduring Faith"** is one that faces all the obstacles that Satan and life may throw your way; to take a page out of the endurance of many believers. Notice that some endured mocking, scourging, and imprisonment. They were made sport

of, they were insulted and cursed. They were beaten with rods, whips and cords of leather straps with bone and metal tied into them, many believers were even killed because of their belief. They were stripped of their possession and treated in the most inhumane ways. Yet they endured and kept the faith and obtained a good report. Hebrews 11:39-3-40

4. **A Staying Faith;** A **"Staying Faith"** is one that stays the course. It is a faith that continues to the very end. It is a faith that does not waver in the face of adversity. It is a faith that refuses to compromise with the standards of the world. It is not a faith that straddles the fence, it is a faith on the side of God and what Jesus Christ accomplished at Calvary.

5. **A Self-Denying Faith;** We have touched on how Moses denied the pleasures of sin and the household of Pharaoh, but what about his kind of faith for today's believer? Self-denying faith is much deeper than depriving oneself of other things. The greatest example of a **"Self-Denying Faith"** for today can be found within the words of Jesus Christ.

"And he (Jesus) said to them all, (everyone who will listen), If any man will come after Me (this deals with anyone seeking true salvation), let him deny himself (the phrase, "deny himself" is to remove oneself and stop working within our own ability, strength and understanding. In other words, stop trying to serve Him with self efforts, it just will not work), take up his cross daily (the

> *cross that Jesus is speaking of is the Victory that Jesus Christ accomplished (His Finished Works John 19:30) at Calvary, (This must be everyday. You cannot live on yesterday's anointing) and follow me. Luke 9:23 Emphasis Mine*

When you stop trying to do it your way and begin to walk in what has been supplied to you through what Jesus Christ has already accomplished, you will begin to walk in the **"Newness of Life" (Romans 6:4). This will also give the Holy Spirit the latitude to live through you and direct your everyday living! (Romans 8)**

The Apostle Paul instructed the believers in Corinth to live a life of separation from the world;

> *"Be ye not unequally yoked together with unbelievers: for what fellowship hath righteousness with unrighteousness? And what communion hath light with darkness?'*

> *"And what concord hath Christ with Belial? Or what part hath he that believeth with an infidel?'*

> *"And what agreement hath the temple of God with idols? For ye are the temple of the living God; as God hath said, I will dwell in them, and walk in them; and I will be their God, and they shall be my people."*

> *"Wherefore come out from among them, and be ye separate, saith the Lord, and touch not the unclean thing; and I will receive you." 2 Cor. 6:14-17*

The call of the above passage of scripture is for the Christian (Child of God) to come out from the world. It is to separate oneself from entangling themselves with the world and its evil ways. It is sad to say, however, the **'Modern Day Church'** has opened its doors to the world without offering a change in their life. I personally have witnessed churches using the world in on their platform while saying, ***'We have to be culturally relevant!'*** That may be, however, that which is the **'Cross and Christ crucified and resurrected!" (1Cor. 1:17-18, 23)**

I do believe that most Christians really do not understand how to become separated from the world. For many years we have tried everything from A to Z to become separated. The problem is, we have been trying in our own strength, ability and knowledge, and that just does not work. In the great book of Luke chapter 9:23, Jesus said to everyone that would come to Him to **"deny themselves take up his cross and follow Him."** The only way for the believer to begin to **'deny themselves'** is to allow the Holy Spirit to do the work with them. The work that the Holy Spirit does is called, **'Sanctification.' (Romans 8)** Sanctification is separating oneself from the world and being separated to God. It is in three stages;

1. **Initial Sanctification. This took place the moment you received Jesus Christ into your life!**

2. **Progressive (ongoing) Sanctification. This is what is taking place in one's life currently. It is the Holy Spirit working to trim of the things of this world and that includes the selfish desires of our flesh!**

3. **Eternal Sanctification. This takes place when the believer receives their Glorified Body and will forever (eternally) be with the Lord!**

**THE CHALLENGE IS TO LET GO
AND ALLOW THE HOLY SPIRIT TO DO
THE WORK HE CAME TO DO IN YOU!**

CONCLUSION

There is so much to learn from those within the **"Hall of Fame of Faith."** Consider those that we have not mentioned in this small study, such as;

> **Isaac's Faith, which was a Repentant Faith!**
> **Jacob's Faith, which was a Faith of Worship!**
> **Joseph's Faith, which was an Undying Faith!**
> **The Parents of Moses, who had a Loving, Fearless Faith!**
> **Israel's Faith was one of Deliverance and Conquering Faith!**
> **Rahab's Faith was a Saving Faith!**

The Heroic Faith of many Believer's such as:

> **Gideon, Barak, Samson, Jephthah, David, and many others even to those who are Heroes of Faith Today!**

The common thread that ran through each of these in this great chapter was; **"They Looked Toward The Cross of Christ." The believer of today is to look back at (have as their object of faith) The Cross and The Finished Work of Jesus Christ! They lived a life of separation to God!**

ABOUT THE AUTHOR

Dr. Baldock is the founder/president of *"Gaining The Victory Ministries."* He is currently celebrating 51 years of ministry.

Dr. Baldock began his ministry in March of 1971. In March of 1973, he began in full time ministry. He and his wife Julie have been married for thirty-five years. Together they have seven grown children; Rick, Tammy, Tracy, Rhonda, Alicia, Michael and Ashley. He and Julie also have several grandchildren and great-grandchildren.

Dr. Baldock has pastored nine churches; four of which he pioneered and built from the ground floor up. Dr. Baldock also has four earned Doctorate Degrees, and one Honorary Doctorate.

He is currently traveling around to different churches teaching and preaching the word of God. Dr. Baldock currently attends the Sanctuary Church in Beech Grove/ Indianapolis. Dr. Baldock has spoken at many conventions and has worked with several well-known ministries. He taught for several years with the International College of Bible Theology and with Midwest Seminary. He has taught undergraduate and graduate school.

He taught at the School of the Prophets in Poplar Bluff, Missouri for about four years, and he taught about two to three years at The Lion of Judah in Malden, Missouri.

Dr. Baldock also traveled to Malawi in East Africa and, for thirteen days, he and two other ministers trained over one hundred and twenty-five church leaders.

Dr. Baldock is a gifted preacher and teacher of the Word of God. He enjoys helping to restore those who have fallen on hard times and are in need of mentoring. He enjoys working with and training pastors and church leaders.

Dr. Baldock has authored many books and study helps. He believes that the gifts that God has given him should be shared and imparted to others. He believes that every day, practical teaching will reveal the application of the Word of God in the person's everyday living. He is a strong believer in the fact that everything you will ever receive from God is because of the **"Cross"** and **"The finished work of Jesus Christ."**

He believes that the **"Cross"** is the means of all you will ever need, and that **"Jesus Christ is the Source"** of all the provisions of God.

Dr. Baldock is available to speak and teach at your local church or conferences, along with leadership training and motivational speaking. If you would like for Dr. Baldock to come and speak at your church or conference, or if you would like more information about his books, CD's, DVD's and a plethora of teaching tools, you can write to:

Gaining the Victory Ministries, Inc.
Dr. Mike Baldock
P.O. Box 648
Spencer, Indiana 47460

Or, you can e-mail him at;
gainingvictoryministries@gmail.com